Strip-Smart Quilts
16 Designs from One Easy Technique

Kathy Brown

Martingale®
& COMPANY

Strip-Smart Quilts: 16 Designs from One Easy Technique
© 2011 by Kathy Brown

That Patchwork Place® is an imprint of Martingale & Company®.

Martingale & Company
19021 120th Ave. NE, Suite 102
Bothell, WA 98011-9511 USA
www.martingale-pub.com

Library of Congress Cataloging-in-Publication Data is available upon request.

ISBN: 978-1-60468-055-3

Mission Statement

Dedicated to providing quality products and service to inspire creativity.

CREDITS

President & CEO: Tom Wierzbicki
Editor in Chief: Mary V. Green
Managing Editor: Tina Cook
Developmental Editor: Karen Costello Soltys
Technical Editor: Christine Barnes
Copy Editor: Marcy Heffernan
Design Director: Stan Green
Production Manager: Regina Girard
Illustrator: Laurel Strand
Cover & Text Designer: Adrienne Smitke
Photographer: Brent Kane

Printed in China
16 15 14 13 12 11   8 7 6 5 4 3

Dedication

To my dad, Alan Stout, 1923–2010.

A son, brother, husband, father, grandfather, uncle, grandson, nephew, friend, neighbor, scholar, teacher, veteran, mechanical engineer, woodcarver, reader, golfer, musician, scoutmaster, and so much more. But to his only daughter, forever Daddy.

Because her father listened to her, she knew she had something to say.
Because he believed in her, she believed in herself.
Because he said she could do anything, she did.
—Author unknown

Contents

The Secret of GRITS (Girl Raised in the South)

I'm about to let you in on a little secret. Well, a *big* secret. About me. One that I usually don't share with many folks. But I'm about to. In print. For all the world to see. Or at least for all of the *quilting* world to see. I guess you can see that I'm nervous about sharing this secret. *Very* nervous. 'Cause although I'm usually a very open person, there *are* some things a girl just doesn't like to share. But I said I would tell you, so here goes. No more stalling. No more draggin' my feet in the sand—or the bayou in my case.

Sigh. I'm a double agent. I lead a double life. By day, I'm the mild-mannered, rule-following, gentle Southern girl. A girl raised in the south—a GRITS. Taught to say "yes ma'am" and "no ma'am," "yes sir" and "no sir" to those who are as much as an hour older than myself and as young as a baby in the crib. Raised to be polite in all situations, be kind and gentle to all creatures, live by the Golden Rule, respect my elders, follow each and every negative thought toward another human being with "bless her little heart," and above all else—follow the rules. You know, the *rules*. Those all-encompassing guiding principles handed down by our mothers and fathers and scores of other authority figures. Those rules make up who I am. That's me, to a T.

But there's another side of me. A darker side that usually comes out at night, when I'm alone and I don't have to worry that someone might catch a glimpse of this quirky, creative, rule-breaking side of me. And on these nights, I begin to laugh. A half-crazed, gleeful laugh. And I am set free. Free to go hog wild and crazy. Free to break the rules. No, not *all* of the rules. After all, I *am* a true Southern girl. I'm talking about the *other* rules. You know, the "quilting rules." The ones that have been handed down by generations of quilters. The ones that tell you that you *must* iron your seam allowances in a particular direction or that you *must* wash your fabrics before using them. The ones that tell you that you *must*, you *must*, you *must*! *Those rules.* Those are the ones this impatient, can't-wait-for-anything quilter believes should be challenged. Those are the rules I break. And I'm not ashamed. I break until I can break no more, and it is a good thing. And it is—for me—life changing. I piece and I quilt. And I do so with a smile on my face and joy in my heart.

Sigh. So the time has come. Sooner or later the truth had to be told. And by telling you, right here and now, I've been set free. Free to break the quilting rules anytime and anywhere I want. And it feels right, sharing this secret with you. So that *you too* can be set free. Free to break the quilting rules. Without worry and without fear. And together, we can piece. And we can quilt. And we can have a smile on our faces and joy in our hearts.

One Ruler + One Triangle = Quilting FUN!

Throughout my quilting life, I've tried to figure out an easier way of accomplishing my goals. And as you know by now, I am the quintessential impatient quilter. I love, love, love, *love* the look of intricate quilts, but the creative side of me is forever searching for a faster way to make these wonderful quilts.

Enter the Creative Grids rulers. Discovering these special rulers has forever transformed my view of rulers in general. You see, up until now, I considered rulers a necessary evil. Kind of like buying tires for your car. You have to have them to make the car move, but you sure hate to pay for a new set because, well, there are other things to spend money on. Like fabric!

Well, I looked at rulers in much the same way. I needed to have a couple of good rulers to cut my fabrics accurately, but I sure didn't need them for anything else. Nope, no specialty rulers for me. I could see no purpose for them in my quilting endeavors.

And then it happened. I lost all reason one day. Can't say what brought it on, or why, but it happened. As I look back on it, I figure it must have been some kind of divine intervention, 'cause I certainly was not myself when I picked up a set of specialty rulers by Creative Grids and brought them home. Home. To my ruler basket. And there they sat, alone and unused, for several months. Until that divine intervention thing happened again. And it couldn't have happened at a worse time. Since my work schedule was bursting at the seams, I decided I needed a break before I broke from the stress. What led me to that ruler basket I will never know, but there I went. And I picked up one of the rulers. A funny-looking

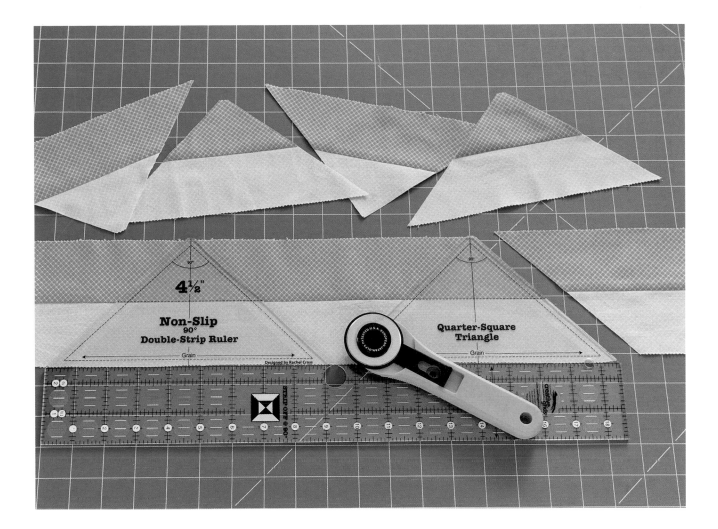

thing, with angles on one side and a straight edge on the other. I guess the uniqueness of the shape caught my eye.

Unwrapping the 90° Double-Strip ruler and glancing at the instructions, I found a fun, intricate block that could be made from just one cut of the ruler. And that's all it took. My mind started racing, and I knew that I would never be content just making a quilt from the block shown in the directions. It's that rule-breaking need that I have.

Out came a brand-spanking-new sketchbook and a new pencil, and my fingers were flying faster than the wind. I looked up a bit later only to realize I'd been drawing for more than three hours and had designed more than 30 quilts with this wondrous new ruler! Easy, quick, spectacular quilts that looked, in some cases, very intricate

but would be so very simple to construct with this ruler. So I reached into my stash, brought out some fabrics, and set out to play. Just one ruler and one triangle shape were all I needed to have fun. And I pieced. And I quilted. And it *was* fun—lots and lots and lots of fun! And as I worked, I did so with a smile on my face and joy in my heart.

I chose 16 of those 30-plus designs to share with you in the hope that you, too, will be set free to quilt and have fun. And, right here and now, I challenge you to break the rules! Make any one of these quilts, and having made it, make another. But this time, rearrange the blocks, mix things up, change the fabrics. Whatever strikes your fancy, go for it. And as you do, I'm sure I'll catch a glimpse of you doing it with a smile on *your* face, and joy in *your* heart!

Quiltmaking Rule-Breaking Basics

Successful strip-smart quilts require a few basic supplies and simple instructions. Follow the guidelines (notice I did not say *rules*) below as you construct your quilts.

Materials

Quilt-shop fabrics
Thread in a neutral color
Rotary cutter
24" x 36" cutting mat or larger
Creative Grids 90° Double-Strip ruler CGRDBS90
6" square ruler
Spray starch
Pins
Sewing machine in good working order
    with a ¼" presser foot
Seam ripper

Rotary Cutting

Since rotary cutting is a topic covered in so many quilting books, I won't go into detail on how to use a rotary cutter here. You do, however, need to start each project with a new rotary-cutter blade. You'll be cutting through the seams of strip sets and will need the sharp, accurate edge a new blade provides.

The quilts in this book use a variety of strip combinations to make the strip sets needed:

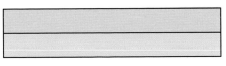

2½" strip + 2½" strip

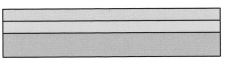

1½" strip + 1½" strip + 2½" strip

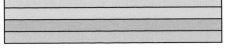

1½" strip + 1½" strip + 1½" strip + 1½" strip

STARCH FOR SUCCESS

The quilts in this book use precut strips and yardage found in quilt shops. Before rotary cutting with the 90° Double-Strip ruler I advise starching the fabric to stabilize it. The cuts you make with this ruler produce bias edges, and starch helps prevent these edges from stretching. If the quilts require precut 2½"-wide strips, which typically come from Jelly Rolls, it's not necessary to starch the strips prior to sewing. But do press your strip sets after sewing them. Take care to press straight and do not stretch the sets by twisting or turning the iron. A simple up-and-down, side-to-side motion will ensure straight sets.

CUTTING TRIANGLES

Rotary cutting using the 90° Double-Strip ruler is simple, fast, and accurate. Follow the guidelines below for left-hand or right-hand cutting; ruler placement remains the same.

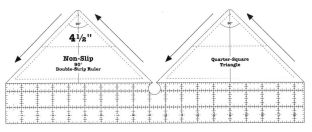

Right-hand cutting follows the ruler from right to left.

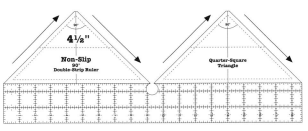

Left-hand cutting follows the ruler from left to right.

1. Lay your strip ruler down on top of a strip set (strip set right side up), lining up the left edge of the ruler approximately 1" to the right of the beginning of the strip set, the bottom edge of the triangles on the ruler with the bottom edge of the strip set, and the middle dashed line on the ruler with the middle seam line of the strip set.

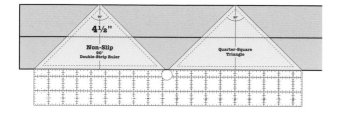

2. Cut your first set of triangles—three in all. If the strip set was made from fat quarters, you've cut all the triangles you can from this set. Rotate the next fat-quarter strip set 180° before cutting so that the fabric strip that was along the top in the first strip set is now along the bottom.

   If the strip set was made from 42"-long strips, the remainder of your strip set will look something like that shown below. Proceed to the next step.

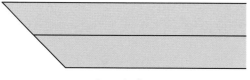

Remainder

3. Rotate the remainder of the strip set 180° so the fabric strip that was along the top is now along the bottom. Once again, lay your strip ruler down on top of the strip set, this time lining up the *right* sloping edge of the ruler with the cut angle of the strip set, the bottom edge of the triangles on the ruler with the bottom edge of the strip set, and the middle dashed seam line on the ruler with the middle

seam line of the strip set. Cut out a second set of triangles.

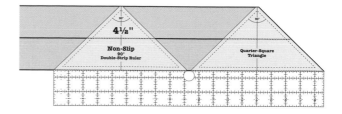

Illustrated below are the triangle shapes that will result from one strip set made from yardage or precut 2½" x 42" strips, or two strip sets made from fat quarters.

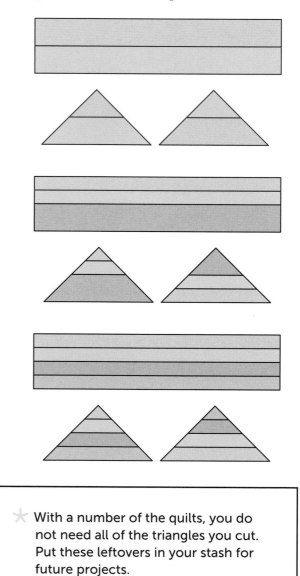

★ With a number of the quilts, you do not need all of the triangles you cut. Put these leftovers in your stash for future projects.

SUB-CUTTING TRIANGLES

For several of the quilts in this book you'll need to cut the triangles created with the 90° Double-Strip ruler in half to make pairs of smaller, mirror-image 90° triangles.

1. Cut triangles as described in "Cutting Triangles" on page 11.
2. Lay a 90° triangle face up on your cutting mat. Place a 6" square ruler on the triangle, lining up the bottom edge of the ruler with the bottom raw edge of the triangle, and the right edge of the 6" ruler with the top of the triangle.

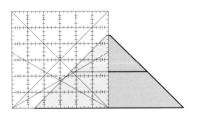

3. Using a rotary cutter, cut the triangle along the edge of the 6" ruler. The result is two mirror-image 90° triangles.

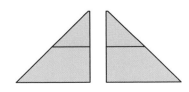

Pinning

To pin or not to pin is an issue most quilters face in their quilting journey. I've found through much trial and error and angst that it is far better *for me* to take the time and pin my blocks to achieve accurate intersecting points, rather than rip the blocks apart when they don't mesh. If perfectly matching seams aren't important to you—that is, if they can be slightly "off" and the resulting look isn't a problem for you—then by all means challenge this rule and break it.

Pressing

Which direction to press the seam allowances on your strip sets is always a consideration. I generally press toward the darker fabric to avoid the show through of color that can occur if you press toward a lighter fabric.

Happily, for many of the quilts in this book, the seam allowances naturally mesh when you join triangle to triangle. In "Penny Candy" (page 62), for example, things work out just fine when joining triangles, because the seam allowances automatically fall in opposite directions.

With "Brownies à la Mode" (page 26), however, the seam allowances will "collide" when you join a red tip/brown strip triangle to another red tip/brown strip triangle. For quilts where this occurs, try this method for pinning the triangles: with right sides together, poke a pin through both triangles exactly at the seam lines. Don't push the pin up and back through the layers, as you would if you were pinning the pieces together to sew. Instead, using the pin to keep the seam lines aligned, pin through all layers ⅛" to the left and ⅛" the right of the poked pin. Then remove the poked pin. Sew the seam slowly, making sure the seam allowances stay flat and smooth.

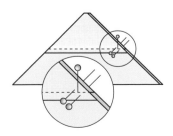

After joining the triangles, press the seam allowances to one side. You'll find that they lie surprisingly flat.

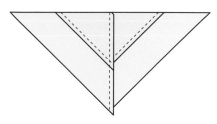

Accurate pressing after piecing your blocks is a must in my opinion. As with pinning, I find that my blocks mesh and are much straighter when I press each seam after sewing. You'll be much happier with your bias edges if you do not challenge this step!

Adding Borders

All but two of the quilts in this book feature borders with butted corners. Cut the border strips across the width of the fabric and piece them as follows to achieve the length needed.

1. Overlap the strips at right angles, with right sides together. Sew diagonally from corner to corner. Trim the excess fabric, leaving a ¼" seam allowance; press the seam allowances open.

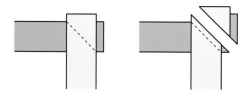

2. Mark the center point on each edge of the quilt top. Mark the center point on one long edge of each border strip. With right sides together, pin the right and left border strips to the quilt top, matching the center points. Note that there will be excess border fabric extending beyond the quilt-top edges. Stitch the borders, and then trim the excess fabric even with the upper and lower edges of the

quilt top. Press the seam allowances toward the border strips. Repeat for the top and bottom borders, trimming the excess even with the sides of the quilt top.

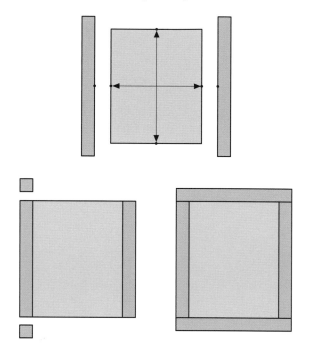

Completing the Quilt

Quilting and binding your quilt are the final steps in the process.

LAYERING AND QUILTING

All of the quilts in this book were quilted on long-arm quilting machines, but you can certainly use any quilting method that you prefer. Before the quilting begins, make sure your backing and batting are at least 4" wider and longer than the quilt top. The yardage requirements in each project have allowed for these extra inches. Layer the batting between the backing (right side down) and the quilt top (right side up), and quilt as desired.

BINDING

Each quilt includes yardage sufficient to cut 2½"-wide binding strips across the width of the fabric.

1. Join the strips with a diagonal seam and trim, leaving a ¼" seam allowance. Press the seam allowances open. Pressing the seam allowances open allows the binding to lie flat when stitched to the quilt. Press the strip in half lengthwise, wrong sides together.

2. Leaving an 8" tail at the beginning, sew the binding to the quilt top using a ¼" seam allowance. Miter the corners as shown.

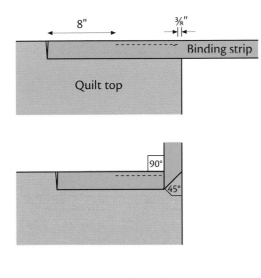

3. Stop sewing when you're about 12" from the beginning; backstitch. Lay the end of the strip over the beginning of the strip. Trim the ends of the strips so they overlap by 2½". Sew the ends together as shown and trim, leaving a ¼" seam allowance. Press the seam allowances open. Reposition the binding on the quilt and finish sewing.

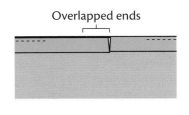

Overlapped ends

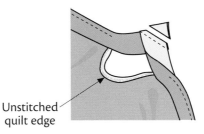

Unstitched quilt edge

4. Fold the edge of the binding to the back of the quilt and hand stitch it down, mitering the corners. I find that the binding folds over the edge more easily if I starch and press it toward the sewn edge.

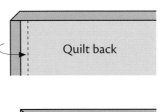

Quilt back

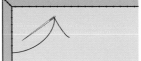

Hide 'n' Seek

Designed by Kathy Brown; pieced by Pam Vieira-McGinnis; quilted by Carol Hilton

Finished Quilt: 58" x 69" ✶ Finished Block: 5½" x 5½"

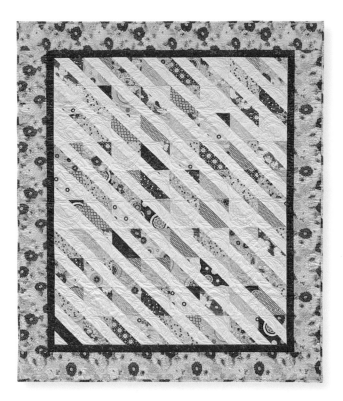

Materials

Yardage is based on 42" wide fabric.

1 Jelly Roll *or* 27 assorted 2½" x 42" strips* of bright florals for blocks

2⅛ yards of white tone-on-tone fabric for blocks

¾ yard of red tone-on-tone fabric for inner border

2⅔ yards of bright floral for outer border and binding

4¼ yards of fabric for backing

66" x 77" piece of batting

In my quilt, I cut one floral strip from the bright floral fabric.

Cutting

From the white tone-on-tone fabric, cut:
27 strips, 2½" x 42"

From the red tone-on-tone fabric, cut:
8 inner-border strips, 2" x 42"

From the bright floral, cut:
8 outer-border strips, 6" x 42"
8 binding strips, 2½" x 42"

Constructing the Blocks

1. With right sides together, sew a white tone-on-tone strip to a bright floral strip. Repeat to make a total of 27 assorted strip sets. Open and starch each strip set as described in "Starch for Success" on page 11.

Make 27 assorted.

2. Referring to "Cutting Triangles" on page 11, cut six 90° double-strip triangles from each strip set.

One of my favorite childhood memories is of playing hide-and-seek. We would gather a group of friends (the more the better), and a rousing game would stretch from house to house, block to block; from the school yard, through the park, and back again. No rules—just play! Hiding behind fences, peeking through the wooden slats, keeping a watchful eye out so you wouldn't be found, caught, and tagged "it"! Oh the excitement, the fun, and the boundless energy that we all had back then.

In designing this quilt, I wanted to capture that feeling of excitement as I silently waited not *to be caught. By choosing bright, bold colors in contrast to stark white, the memory of peeking through those backyard fences came to life. Take a trip back to your childhood and whip up your own version of "Hide 'n' Seek" in no time at all!*

3. Separate the triangles into two sets of 81 triangles each:

   - white tip/floral strip
   - floral tip/white strip

4. With right sides together, sew a white-tip triangle to a floral-tip triangle, varying the floral fabrics. Make 80 blocks. (Note: You'll have one triangle left over from each set.) Starch each block to preserve the bias edges of the triangles.

Make 80.

Assembling the Quilt Top

1. Using a design wall or other flat surface, arrange the completed blocks as shown, making sure that each block is oriented with the white tip in the lower-left corner and the floral tip in the upper-right corner, and that the floral fabrics vary in blocks that touch.

2. Sew the blocks in each row together; press the seam allowances in opposite directions from row to row. Sew the rows together; press the seam allowances in one direction. To stabilize the bias edges of the quilt top, stitch around the perimeter ⅛" from the raw edges.

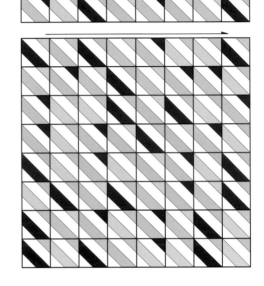

Adding the Borders

1. Referring to "Adding Borders" on page 14, join two inner-border strips to make one long strip. Repeat to make a total of four pieced strips. Sew the inner-border strips to the quilt top; press.

2. Repeat to add the outer-border strips to the quilt top.

Finishing

1. Referring to "Completing the Quilt" on page 14, layer the quilt top with batting and backing. Quilt as desired.

2. Follow the instructions on page 15 to bind the quilt using the 2½"-wide strips.

Daydream Believer

Designed by Kathy Brown; pieced by Linda Reed; quilted by Carol Hilton

Finished quilt: 40" x 48" ★ Finished block: 8" x 8"

It was a warm September night in 1966 when my dad turned on the television so we could watch one of our favorite comedies, Gilligan's Island. Having only two broadcast channels available back then, Dad made the fateful mistake of turning on the channel opposite of Gilligan. Right then and there I lost my heart to four young men who burst onto the television screen and filled the room with song and laughter. From that moment on, The Monkees took over our Monday night television schedule, amid the loud and unrelenting protests of my brothers. As with many a young girl, my bedroom was transformed into a Monkees memorabilia studio, complete with teen magazine "wallpaper" and so many trading cards surrounding my mirror that I could barely see my own image! As I look back, I can only imagine my parents' patience as I listened to "I'm a Believer," "Last Train to Clarksville," and "Daydream Believer" over and over and over and over again—at ear-splitting levels.

As I worked with the design of this quilt, the four pieces that make up a block reminded me of those four young men and the wonderful memories they made in my younger days. I hope this quilt sparks warm memories of your own as well.

Materials

Yardage is based on 42"-wide fabric.

1 yard of cream swirl fabric for blocks
1 yard of green leaf print for blocks
2 yards of medium black floral for blocks
    and binding
2¾ yards of fabric for backing (pieced with a
    horizontal seam)
48" x 56" piece of batting

Cutting

From the cream swirl fabric, cut:
20 strips, 1½" x 42"

From the green leaf print, cut:
20 strips, 1½" x 42"

From the medium black floral, cut:
20 strips, 2½" x 42"
5 binding strips, 2½" x 42"

Constructing the Blocks

1. With right sides together, sew a cream swirl, green leaf, and medium black floral strip into a strip set as shown. Repeat to make a total of 20 cream/green/black strip sets. Open and starch each strip set as described in "Starch for Success" on page 11.

Make 20.

2. Referring to "Cutting Triangles" on page 11, cut six 90° triple-strip triangles from each strip set.

3. Separate the triangles into two sets of 60 triangles each:
   - cream-green tip/black strip
   - black tip/green-cream strip

4. With right sides together, sew 2 cream-green tip/black strip triangles together to make a unit. Repeat to make another unit. Join the units to make one block. Repeat to make a total of 15 blocks. Starch each block to preserve the bias edges of the triangles.

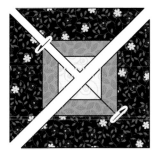

Make 15.

5. Repeat to make 15 black tip/green-cream strip blocks.

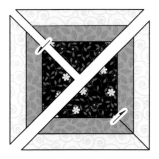

Make 15.

Assembling the Quilt Top

1. Using a design wall or other flat surface, arrange the completed blocks as shown.

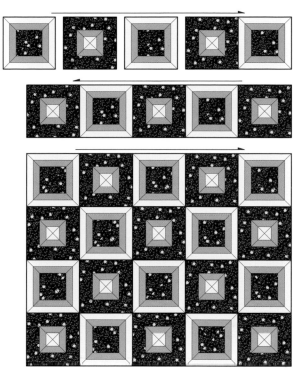

2. Sew the blocks in each row together; press the seam allowances in opposite directions from row to row. Sew the rows together; press the seam allowances in one direction. To stabilize the bias edges of the quilt top, stitch around the perimeter ⅛" from the raw edges.

Finishing

1. Referring to "Completing the Quilt" on page 14, layer the quilt top with batting and backing. Quilt as desired.

2. Follow the instructions on page 15 to bind the quilt using the 2½"-wide strips.

Chinese Jump Rope

Designed by Kathy Brown; pieced by Linda Reed; quilted by Carol Hilton

Finished Quilt: 60" x 71" ★ Finished Block: 11" x 11"

Materials

Yardage is based on 42"-wide fabric.

1⅓ yards of red tone-on-tone fabric for blocks and inner border

¾ yard of gray leaf print for blocks

¾ yard of green leaf print for blocks

¾ yard of black tone-on-tone fabric for blocks

6 yards of tan focus print for blocks, outer border, and binding

4⅓ yards of fabric for backing

68" x 79" piece of batting

Cutting

From the gray leaf print, cut:
14 strips, 1½" x 42"

From the green leaf print, cut:
14 strips, 1½" x 42"

From the black tone-on-tone fabric, cut:
14 strips, 1½" x 42"

From the red tone-on-tone fabric, cut:
14 strips, 1½" x 42"
8 inner-border strips, 2½" x 42"

From the tan focus fabric, cut:
4 outer-border strips, 6½" x 42", from the *crosswise* grain
4 outer-border strips, 6½" x 66", from the *lengthwise* grain
20 squares, 8½" x 8½". Cut each square on point, centering a focus scene.
8 binding strips, 2½" x 42"

Although it pains me to admit it, I was not a very graceful child. Tomboy—yes! Rough and tumble—yes! Graceful—no! Play baseball, football, and kickball; ride bikes; jump rope; golf; play box hockey; and swim—I could do all those with no problem. It was the girlie things that simply were not in me. I've never done a cartwheel or been able to roller skate. I can't do a dance twirl, or heaven forbid, navigate a Chinese jump rope. Just not in me. I envied the girls at school who, hand in hand, could jump into the middle of the Chinese jump ropes, their feet dancing in sync as they laughed and chanted their rhymes. That was an activity I had to watch from the sidelines—until now! A chance purchase of a beautiful Asian focus fabric gave me the perfect opportunity to play "Chinese Jump Rope" my way! Won't you join me?

Constructing the Blocks

1. With right sides together, sew gray, green, red, and black strips into a strip set as shown. Repeat to make a total of 14 gray/green/red/black strip sets. Open and starch each strip set as described in "Starch for Success" on page 11.

Make 14.

2. Following the instructions for "Cutting Triangles" on page 11, cut six 90° multi-strip triangles from each strip set.

3. Separate the triangles into two sets of 42 triangles each:
   - gray-green tip/red-black strip
   - black-red tip/green-gray strip

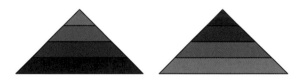

4. With right sides together, sew a black-tip triangle to the upper-left edge of a tan square, and a second identical triangle to the lower-right edge of the square.

5. With right sides together, sew a gray-tip triangle to the upper-right edge of the square, followed by an identical triangle to the lower-left edge of the square. Repeat to make a total of 20 blocks. (Note: You'll have two triangles left over from each set.) Starch each block to preserve the bias edges of the triangles.

Make 20.

6. Sew a straight stitch around the perimeter of each block ⅛" from the raw edges to further stabilize the block.

Assembling the Quilt Top

1. Using a design wall or other flat surface, arrange the blocks as shown.
2. Sew the blocks in each row together; press the seam allowances in opposite directions from row to row. Sew the rows together; press the seam allowances in one direction. To stabilize the bias edges of the quilt top, stitch around the perimeter ⅛" from the raw edges.

Adding the Borders

1. Referring to "Adding Borders" on page 14, join two inner-border strips to make one long strip. Repeat to make a total of four pieced strips. Sew the inner-border strips to the quilt top; press.
2. Repeat to add the outer-border strips to the quilt top.

Finishing

1. Referring to "Completing the Quilt" on page 14, layer the quilt top with batting and backing. Quilt as desired.
2. Follow the instructions on page 15 to bind the quilt using the 2½"-wide strips.

Brownies à la Mode

Designed by Kathy Brown; pieced by Linda Reed; quilted by Carol Hilton

Finished Quilt: 56" x 72" ★ Finished Block: 8" x 8"

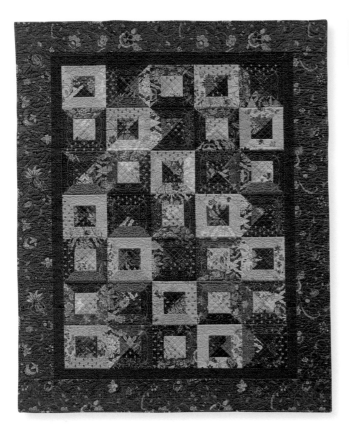

I grew up in the '60s when television shows like Mission Impossible, I Spy, *and* The Man from U.N.C.L.E. *were all the rage. Every night after dinner, we would gather in the family room to watch one of these shows and be transported into the world of spies. As we settled into our favorite places, Dad would invariably ask if there were any "DS." Mom would nod yes or shake her head no, but we were clueless as to what they were talking about. Some nights during commercial breaks, Mom would disappear into the kitchen and reappear with fresh popcorn, fudgy brownies, warm cookies, or even bowls of homemade ice cream. I'm not sure how long it was before we figured out that Dad's code word for dessert was "DS," but we made sure we didn't break the code for fear of losing those treats during TV time!*

The colors in this rich quilt remind me of Mom's fudge brownies. They were a favorite in our family, and I'm sure this quilty remembrance will become a favorite in your household as well!

Materials

Yardage is based on 42"-wide fabric.

16 strips of assorted tan fabrics, 2½" x 42", for blocks

16 strips of assorted deep red fabrics, 2½" x 42", for blocks

16 strips of assorted chocolate brown fabrics, 2½" x 42", for blocks

¾ yard of red tone-on-tone fabric for inner border

2¼ yards of chocolate floral for outer border and binding

4½ yards of fabric for backing

64" x 80" piece of batting

Cutting

From the red tone-on-tone fabric, cut:
8 inner-border strips, 2½" x 42"

From the chocolate floral, cut:
8 outer-border strips, 6½" x 42"
8 binding strips, 2½" x 42"

Constructing the Blocks

1. With right sides together, sew a tan strip to a red strip. Repeat to make a total of eight tan/red strip sets. Make a total of eight tan/chocolate brown strip sets and eight red/chocolate brown strip sets. Open and starch each strip set as described in "Starch for Success" on page 11.

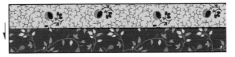

Make 8.

Make 8.

Make 8.

2. Referring to "Cutting Triangles" on page 11, cut six 90° double-strip triangles from each strip set.

3. Separate the triangles into six sets of 24 triangles each:

    -   tan tip/red strip
    -   red tip/tan strip
    -   tan tip/brown strip
    -   brown tip/tan strip
    -   red tip/brown strip
    -   brown tip/red strip

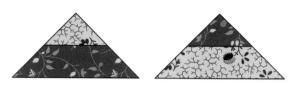

4. Choose four triangles from the same set, but with varied prints. With right sides together, join two triangles to make a unit. Repeat to make another unit. Join the units to make one block.

Make 6.

5. Repeat to make a total of six blocks from the first five triangle sets and five blocks from the last triangle set, for a total of 35 blocks. (Note: You'll have four brown tip/red strip triangles left over.) Starch each block to preserve the bias edges of the triangles.

Make 6.

Make 6.   Make 6.

Make 6.   Make 6.

Assembling the Quilt Top

1. Using a design wall or other flat surface, arrange the completed blocks as shown.
2. Sew the blocks in each row together; press the seam allowances in opposite directions from row to row. Sew the rows together; press the seam allowances in one direction. To stabilize the bias edges of the quilt top, stitch around the perimeter ⅛" from the raw edges.

Adding the Borders

1. Referring to "Adding Borders" on page 14, join two inner-border strips to make one strip. Repeat to make a total of four pieced strips. Sew the inner borders to the quilt top; press.
2. Repeat to add the outer-border strips to the quilt top.

Finishing

1. Referring to "Completing the Quilt" on page 14, layer the quilt top with batting and backing. Quilt as desired.
2. Follow the instructions on page 15 to bind the quilt using the 2½"-wide strips.

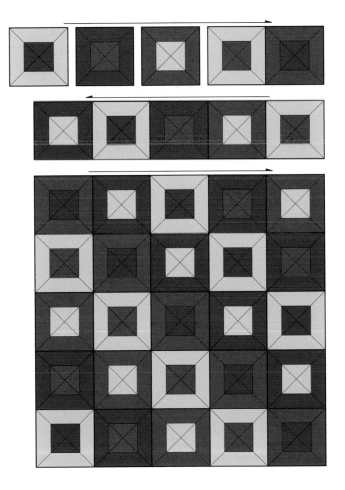

Fat Man's Squeeze

Designed by Kathy Brown; pieced by Kathy Brown and Janell Crosslin; quilted by Carol Hilton

Finished Quilt: 43" x 53" ★ Finished Block: 10" x 10"

Materials

Yardage is based on 42"-wide fabric.

One Jelly Roll *or* 32 assorted red, light blue,
cream*, tan, and navy print 2½" x 42" strips
for blocks
¾ yard of navy print for inner border
2⅛ yards of cream floral for outer border and
binding
2⅞ yards of fabric for backing (pieced with a
horizontal seam)
51" x 61" piece of batting

*In my quilt, I cut one cream strip from the cream
floral fabric.*

Cutting

From the navy print, cut:
8 inner-border strips, 2" x 42"

From the cream floral, cut:
8 outer-border strips, 5½" x 42"
8 binding strips, 2½" x 42"

One of our beloved family vacations took us to visit
relatives in the Great Smoky Mountains of Tennes-
see. On our way to Nashville, we stopped at Rock
City in Chattanooga on top of Lookout Mountain.
There we got to hike up the mountain, see seven
states all at once, walk the Enchanted Trails, visit
Ruby Falls, watch Dad walk across the famous
swinging bridge, and, best of all, go through Fat
Man's Squeeze. As young children, my brothers and
I were amazed at the ancient rock formations that
towered above us. Descending deep into one of the
formations, we held our breaths and "squeezed"
through two immense rocks that threatened to hold
us and not let go. Once through the passage, our
rallying cries of "let's do it again, let's do it again"
must have driven our parents crazy, but they never
let on. The centers of the blocks in this quilt remind
me of that narrow passage in Fat Man's Squeeze—
and a vacation I'll never forget.

Assembling the Strip Sets

1. From the Jelly Roll or your assorted strips, choose:
   - 4 assorted red strips
   - 4 assorted light blue strips
   - 8 assorted tan strips
   - 8 assorted navy blue strips
   - 8 assorted cream strips

2. With right sides together, sew a red strip to a tan strip. Repeat to make a total of four strip sets. Repeat to make a total of four tan/navy strip sets, four cream/navy strip sets, and four cream/light blue strip sets. Open and starch each strip set as described in "Starch for Success" on page 11.

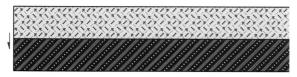

Make 4.

Make 4.

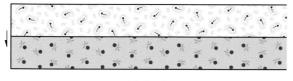

Make 4.

Make 4.

Cutting and Organizing the Triangles

1. Referring to "Cutting Triangles" on page 11, cut six 90° double-strip triangles from each strip set. Sub-cut these triangles into smaller,

mirror-image triangles as instructed in "Sub-Cutting Triangles" on page 13.

2. Separate the triangles into 16 sets of 12 triangles each:
   - tan tip/red strip pointing left
   - tan tip/red strip pointing right
   - red tip/tan strip pointing left
   - red tip/tan strip pointing right
   - tan tip/navy strip pointing left
   - tan tip/navy strip pointing right
   - navy tip/tan strip pointing left
   - navy tip/tan strip pointing right
   - cream tip/navy strip pointing left
   - cream tip/navy strip pointing right
   - navy tip/cream strip pointing left
   - navy tip/cream strip pointing right
   - cream tip/light blue strip pointing left
   - cream tip/light blue strip pointing right
   - light blue tip/cream strip pointing left
   - light blue tip/cream strip pointing right

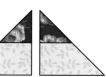
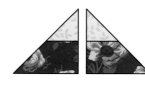

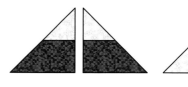

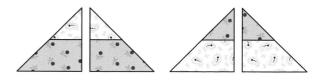

Constructing the Blocks

1. With right sides together, sew a tan tip/red strip pointing left triangle to a red tip/tan strip pointing right triangle. Repeat to make a second unit. Sew the two units together to make a square. Repeat to make a second square.

Make 2.

2. With right sides together, sew a red tip/tan strip pointing left triangle to a tan tip/red strip pointing right triangle. Repeat to make a second unit. Sew the two units together to make a square. Repeat to make a second square. Rotate each of these squares 90° to the right.

Make 2.
Rotate 90°.

3. Working on your design wall or other flat surface, place the two squares from step 1 in the upper-left position and lower-right position. Place the two squares you rotated in step 2 in the upper-right and lower-left positions. Sew the top squares together, and then sew the bottom squares together. Sew the top unit to the bottom unit to make one block. Repeat steps 1–3 to make a total of three red/tan blocks. Starch each block to preserve the bias edges of the triangles.

Make 3.

4. Using the illustrations below as a guide, repeat to make a total of three tan/navy blocks, three cream/navy blocks, and three cream/light blue blocks.

Make 3.

Make 3.

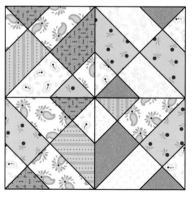

Make 3.

Assembling the Quilt Top

1. Using a design wall or other flat surface, arrange the completed blocks as shown, making sure that each block is oriented correctly.

2. Sew the blocks in each row together; press the seam allowances in opposite directions from row to row. Sew the rows together; press the seam allowances in one direction. To stabilize the bias edges of the quilt top, stitch around the perimeter ⅛" from the raw edges.

Adding the Borders

1. Referring to "Adding Borders" on page 14, join two inner-border strips to make one long strip. Repeat to make a total of four pieced strips. Sew the inner-border strips to the quilt top; press.
2. Repeat to add the outer-border strips to the quilt top.

Finishing

1. Referring to "Completing the Quilt" on page 14, layer the quilt top with batting and backing. Quilt as desired.
2. Follow the instructions on page 15 to bind the quilt using the 2½"-wide strips.

Read All About It!

Designed by Kathy Brown; pieced by Linda Reed; quilted by Carol Hilton

Finished Quilt: 46" x 57" ★ Finished Block: 5½" x 5½"

Materials

Yardage is based on 42"-wide fabric.

1⅓ yards of black leaf print for blocks
1⅓ yards of white bird print for blocks
1 yard of red tone-on-tone fabric for blocks and
    inner border
2⅞ yards of black scroll print for blocks, outer
    border, and binding
3 yards of fabric for backing (pieced with a
    horizontal seam)
54" x 65" piece of batting

Cutting

From the black leaf print, cut:
16 strips, 2½" x 42"

From the white bird print, cut:
16 strips, 2½" x 42"

From the red tone-on-tone fabric, cut:
8 strips, 2½" x 42"
8 inner-border strips, 1½" x 42"

From the black scroll print, cut:
8 strips, 2½" x 42"
8 outer-border strips, 6" x 42"
8 binding strips, 2½" x 42"

Constructing the Blocks

1. With right sides together, sew a black leaf strip to a white bird strip. Repeat to make a total of 16 black leaf/white bird strip sets. Sew a black scroll strip to a red tone-on-tone strip. Repeat to make a total of eight black scroll/red tone-on-tone strip sets. Open and starch each strip set as described in "Starch for Success" on page 11.

Make 16.

Make 8.

"What's black, white, and read all over?" As a little prankster, I would eagerly ask a captive audience (parents, grandparents, aunts, uncles, and scores of other "unsuspecting and unknowing" adults) this question over and over. Of course, since none of them knew the answer (yeah, right!), I would scream "a newspaper!" and dissolve into peals of laughter. Oh to be that young again, when the thrill of telling an age-old joke brought such pleasure.

The blacks, whites, and reds all over this bold quilt remind me of carefree days filled with silly jokes, tongue twisters, and pesky pranks played on patient adults. I hope making it will bring you joy as well.

2. Referring to "Cutting Triangles" on page 11, cut six 90° double-strip triangles from each strip set.

3. Separate the triangles into three sets. (Note: All 24 of the black scroll tip/red tone-on-tone strip triangles will be left over.)
   - 48 white bird tip/black leaf strip
   - 48 black leaf tip/white bird strip
   - 24 red tone-on-tone tip/black scroll strip

4. With right sides together, sew a black leaf–tip triangle to a white bird–tip triangle. Repeat to make a total of 24 blocks. (Note: You'll have 24 white bird tip/black leaf strip triangles left over.)

Make 24.

5. With right sides together, sew a black leaf–tip triangle to a red tone-on-tone–tip triangle. Repeat to make a total of 24 blocks. Starch each block to preserve the bias edges of the triangles.

Make 24.

Assembling the Quilt Top

1. Using a design wall or other flat surface, arrange the completed blocks as shown.

2. Sew the blocks in each row together; press the seam allowances in opposite directions from row to row. Sew the rows together; press the seam allowances in one direction. To stabilize the bias edges of the quilt top, stitch around the perimeter ⅛" from the raw edges.

Adding the Borders

1. Referring to "Adding Borders" on page 14, join two inner-border strips to make one long strip. Repeat to make a total of four pieced strips. Sew the inner-border strips to the quilt top; press.

2. Repeat to add the outer-border strips to the quilt top.

Finishing

1. Referring to "Completing the Quilt" on page 14, layer the quilt top with batting and backing. Quilt as desired.

2. Follow the instructions on page 15 to bind the quilt using the 2½"-wide strips.

The Birds

Designed by Kathy Brown; pieced by Linda Reed; quilted by Carol Hilton

Finished Quilt: 57" x 72" ★ Finished Block: 10½" x 10½"

I was about nine years old when I saw my very first really scary movie. Alfred Hitchcock's The Birds *came on television, and I was spellbound. Too scared to cover my eyes, too absorbed to turn away! To this day, when I see a murder of crows I think back to that movie and the fascination it held for me. This quilt, featuring quite different birds, is a pleasant and decidedly* not *scary depiction of* The Birds.

Materials

Yardage is based on 42"-wide fabric.

½ yard *each* of light gold and dark gold prints for blocks

½ yard *each* of light cream and dark cream prints for blocks

½ yard *each* of light tan and dark tan prints for blocks

½ yard *each* of light green and dark green prints for blocks

4¼ yards of bird print for solid squares, border, and binding

1 yard chocolate brown print for corner and side setting triangles

4½ yards of fabric for backing

65" x 80" piece of batting

Cutting

From *each* of the light gold, dark gold, light cream, dark cream, light tan, dark tan, light green, and dark green prints, cut:

8 strips, 1½" x 42"

From the bird print, fussy cut:

6 squares, 11" x 11"; cut each square on point and centered on a bird or birds

From the bird print, also cut:

8 border strips, 6½" x 42"

8 binding strips, 2½" x 42"

From the chocolate brown print, cut:

2 squares, 8" x 8"; cut each square in half diagonally to yield 4 corner setting triangles

3 squares, 16" x 16"; cut each square into quarters diagonally to yield 12 side setting triangles

Assembling the Strip Sets

1. With right sides together, sew dark gold, dark cream, dark green, and dark tan strips into a strip set as shown. Repeat to make a total of eight strip sets. Open and starch each strip set as described in "Starch for Success" on page 11.

Make 8.

2. With right sides together, sew light gold, light cream, light tan, and light green strips into a strip set as shown.

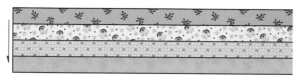

Make 8.

Cutting and Organizing the Triangles

1. Referring to "Cutting Triangles" on page 11, cut six 90° double-strip triangles from each strip set. Cut each triangle in half to make two smaller, mirror-image triangles as instructed in "Sub-Cutting Triangles" on page 13.

2. Separate the triangles into eight sets of 24 triangles each. Label the sets of dark and light triangles as shown:
   - dark A, dark B, dark C, dark D
   - light A, light B, light C, light D

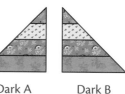

Dark A   Dark B

Dark C   Dark D

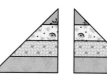

Light A   Light B

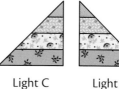

Light C   Light D

Constructing the Blocks

Refer to the illustrations to place the triangles on a design wall or other flat surface to ensure correct placement prior to sewing.

1. With right sides together, sew a dark A triangle to a dark C triangle, orienting the triangles as shown. Follow with a dark C triangle to a dark A triangle. Sew the AC unit to

the CA unit. Repeat to make a total of 12 AC squares.

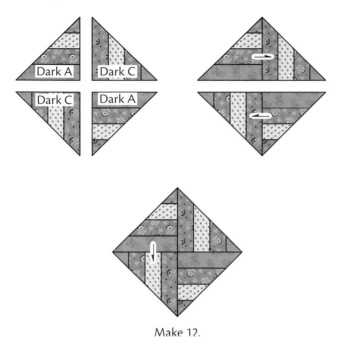

Make 12.

2. With right sides together, sew a dark B triangle to a dark D triangle. Follow with a dark D triangle to a dark B triangle. Sew the BD unit to the DB unit. Repeat to make a total of 12 BD squares.

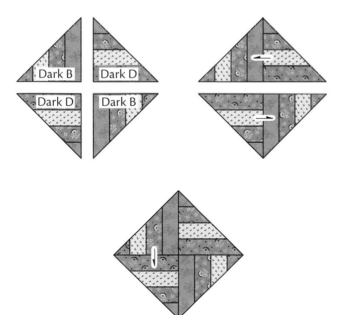

Make 12.

3. With right sides together, sew a dark AC square to a dark BD square. Sew a dark BD square to a dark AC square. Sew the two units together to make a Four Patch block. Repeat this process to make a total of six dark blocks. Starch each block to preserve the bias edges of the triangles.

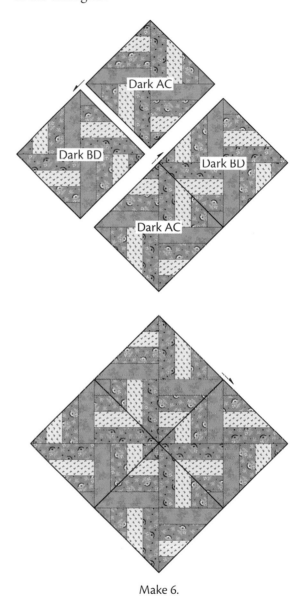

Make 6.

4. Repeat the process to make a total of six light blocks using triangles with the same letter designations as the dark blocks.

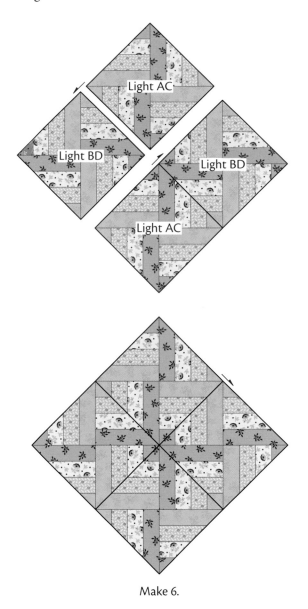

Make 6.

Assembling the Quilt Top

1. Using a design wall or other flat surface, arrange the pieced blocks, solid squares, and setting triangles as shown.

2. Sew the blocks, solid squares, and side setting triangles in each diagonal row together. (Note: You'll have two side setting triangles left over.) Press the seam allowances toward the solid squares and the setting triangles.

3. Sew the rows together. Press the seam allowances in one direction.

4. Add the corner setting triangles. Press the seam allowances toward the triangles. To stabilize the bias edges of the quilt top, stitch around the perimeter ⅛" from the raw edges.

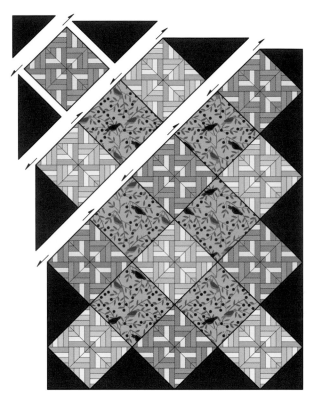

Adding the Borders

Referring to "Adding Borders" on page 14, join two border strips to make one long strip. Repeat to make a total of four pieced strips. Sew the border strips to the quilt top; press.

Finishing

1. Referring to "Completing the Quilt" on page 14, layer the quilt top with batting and backing. Quilt as desired.

2. Follow the instructions on page 15 to bind the quilt using the 2½"-wide strips.

Merry-Go-Round

Designed by Kathy Brown; pieced by the Southern Ladies Quilting Society; quilted by Carol Hilton

Finished Quilt: 71" x 82" ★ Finished Block: 5½" x 5½"

Materials

Yardage is based on 42"-wide fabric.

One Jelly Roll *or* 40 assorted 2½" x 42" strips
   of florals for blocks
3 yards of white tone-on-tone fabric for blocks
¾ yard of blue tone-on-tone fabric for inner
   border
2¼ yards of multicolored floral for outer border
   and binding
5 yards of fabric for backing
79" x 90" piece of batting

Cutting

From the white tone-on-tone fabric, cut:
40 strips, 2½" x 42"

From the blue tone-on-tone fabric, cut:
8 inner-border strips, 2½" x 42"

From the multicolored floral, cut:
8 outer-border strips, 6½" x 42"
8 binding strips, 2½" x 42"

Constructing the Blocks

1. With right sides together, sew an assorted
   floral strip to a white tone-on-tone strip.
   Repeat to make a total of 40 assorted floral/
   white tone-on-tone strip sets. Open and
   starch each strip set as described in "Starch
   for Success" on page 11.

Make 40 assorted.

2. Referring to "Cutting Triangles" on page 11,
   cut six 90° double-strip triangles from each
   strip set.

*I grew up in a fantastic community of caring neigh-
bors where everyone knew everybody. We had the
bonus of an elementary school and neighborhood
park across the street from our home. The park
was my favorite place to go, with swings that took
you to the sky and back, slides that seemed 100 feet
high, and huge oak trees to lie under while star-
ing at the clouds and daydreaming. It was a safe,
secure spot—with one exception. A monster lived
in the merry-go-round, and he appeared every
time I hopped on to ride, leaving me dizzy and
unable to see straight or walk. I so envied the other
kids who could ride forever and never meet that
terrible creature.*

   *This quilt reminds me of that merry-go-round,
spinning from the center outward—but without the
dreaded monster. A nice, safe ride!*

3. Separate the triangles into two sets of 120 triangles each:
    - white tone-on-tone tip/floral strip
    - floral tip/white tone-on-tone strip

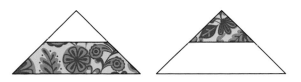

4. With right sides together, sew a floral-tip triangle to a white tone-on-tone–tip triangle. Repeat to make a total of 120 blocks. Starch each block to preserve the bias edges of the triangles.

Make 120 assorted.

Assembling the Quilt Top

1. Using a design wall or other flat surface, arrange the completed blocks as shown.

2. Sew the blocks in each row together; press the seam allowances in opposite directions from row to row. Sew the rows together; press the seam allowances in one direction. To stabilize the bias edges of the quilt top, stitch around the perimeter ⅛" from the raw edges.

Adding the Borders

1. Referring to "Adding Borders" on page 14, join two inner-border strips to make one long strip. Repeat to make a total of four pieced strips. Sew the inner-border strips to the quilt top; press.
2. Repeat to add the outer-border strips to the quilt top.

Finishing

1. Referring to "Completing the Quilt" on page 14, layer the quilt top with batting and backing. Quilt as desired.
2. Follow the instructions on page 15 to bind the quilt using the 2½"-wide strips.

The Twist

Designed by Kathy Brown; pieced by Linda Reed; quilted by Carol Hilton

Finished Quilt: 54¼" x 70¾" ★ Finished Block: 7¼" x 7¼"

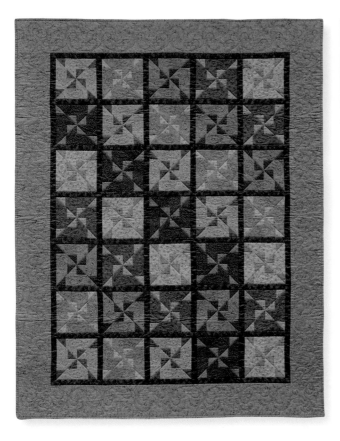

The first dance move I ever learned, at the ripe old age of five, was the twist. I would listen to Chubby Checker belt out "The Twist" and "Let's Twist Again" over and over on Mom and Dad's LPs as I danced my little heart out. The songs during that era were such fun, and they bring back many happy memories. When I first made this Twist block, it reminded me of the times way back when, and how I loved to twist the night away!

Materials

Yardage is based on 42"-wide fabric.

2⅞ yards of medium tan floral for blocks, outer border, and binding
¾ yard of light tan floral for blocks
¾ yard of dark tan florals for blocks
¾ yard *each* of light, medium, and dark gray florals for blocks
1 yard of charcoal gray fabric for inner border and sashing
4 yards of fabric for backing
61" x 77" piece of batting

Cutting

From *each* of the light, medium, and dark tan florals and *each* of the light, medium, and dark gray florals, cut:
8 strips, 2½" x 42"

From the medium tan floral, also cut:
8 outer-border strips, 6½" x 42"
8 binding strips, 2½" x 42"

From the charcoal gray fabric, cut:
28 sashing strips, 1½" x 7¾"
6 sashing strips, 1½" x 41"
8 inner-border strips, 1½" x 42"

Assembling the Strip Sets

With right sides together, sew a light tan strip to a light gray strip. Repeat to make a total of 8 strip sets. Make a total of 8 medium tan/medium gray strip sets, and 8 dark tan/dark gray strip sets. Open and starch each strip set as described in "Starch for Success" on page 11.

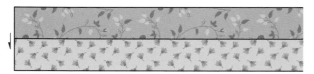

Make 8.

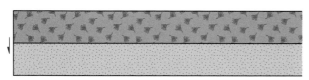

Make 8.

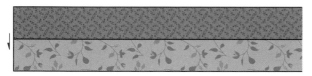

Make 8.

Cutting and Organizing the Triangles

1. Referring to "Cutting Triangles" on page 11, cut six 90° double-strip triangles from each strip set. Cut each triangle in half to make two smaller, mirror-image triangles as instructed in "Sub-Cutting Triangles" on page 13.

2. Separate the triangles into 12 sets of 24 triangles each:
   - light tan tip/light gray strip pointing left
   - light tan tip/light gray strip pointing right
   - light gray tip/light tan strip pointing left
   - light gray tip/light tan strip pointing right
   - medium tan tip/medium gray strip pointing left
   - medium tan tip/medium gray strip pointing right
   - medium gray tip/medium tan strip pointing left
   - medium gray tip/medium tan strip pointing right
   - dark tan tip/dark gray strip pointing left
   - dark tan tip/dark gray strip pointing right
   - dark gray tip/dark tan strip pointing left
   - dark gray tip/dark tan strip pointing right

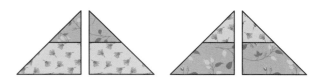

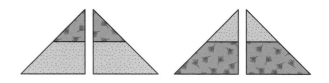

Constructing the Blocks

Refer to the illustrations and arrange the triangles on a design wall or other flat surface to ensure correct placement prior to sewing.

1. With right sides together, sew a light tan tip/light gray strip pointing left triangle to a light tan tip/light gray strip pointing left triangle. Repeat to make a total of 4 units. Sew the units together to make one block. Repeat to make a total of 3 blocks. Starch each block to preserve the bias edges of the triangles.

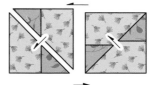

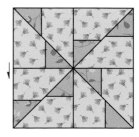

Make 3.

2. Using the block illustrations below, repeat to make a total of 3 blocks from each triangle set. (Note: You'll use 35 blocks.) Starch each block to preserve the bias edges of the triangles.

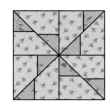

Make 3.

Make 3.

Make 3.

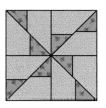

Make 3.

Make 3.

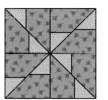

Make 3.

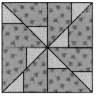

Make 3.

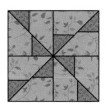

Make 3.

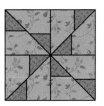

Make 3.

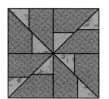

Make 3.

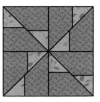

Make 3.

Assembling the Quilt Top

1. Using a design wall or other flat surface, arrange the completed blocks and sashing strips as shown.
2. Sew the blocks and 7¾"-long sashing strips in each row together; press the seam allowances toward the sashing strips. Sew the rows and the 41"-long sashing strips together, trimming the strips to fit. Press the seam allowances toward the sashing strips.

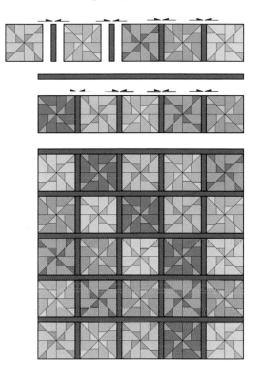

Adding the Borders

1. Referring to "Adding Borders" on page 14, join two inner-border strips to make one long strip. Repeat to make a total of four pieced strips. Sew the inner-border strips to the quilt top; press.
2. Repeat to add the outer-border strips to the quilt top.

Finishing

1. Referring to "Completing the Quilt" on page 14, layer the quilt top with batting and backing. Quilt as desired.
2. Follow the instructions on page 15 to bind the quilt using the 2½"-wide strips.

Pedal Pushers

Designed by Kathy Brown; pieced by the Southern Ladies Quilting Society; quilted by Carol Hilton

Finished Quilt: 44" x 54" ★ Finished Block: 5" x 5"

Materials

Yardage is based on 42"-wide fabric.

One Jelly Roll *or* 32 assorted pink. blue, green, yellow, cream, peach, and eggplant print strips, 2½" x 42", for blocks

½ yard of green print for inner border

2 yards of cream floral for outer border and binding

3 yards of fabric for backing (pieced with a horizontal seam)

52" x 62" piece of batting

Cutting

From the green print, cut:
6 inner-border strips, 2½" x 42"

From the cream floral, cut:
8 outer-border strips, 5½" x 42"
8 binding strips, 2½" x 42"

Assembling the Strip Sets

1. From the Jelly Roll, choose:
   - 2 assorted eggplant strips
   - 4 assorted peach strips
   - 4 assorted yellow strips
   - 4 assorted light blue strips
   - 4 assorted green strips
   - 6 assorted pink strips
   - 8 assorted cream strips

2. With right sides together, sew a cream strip to a pink strip. Repeat to make a total of 4 strip sets.

To a kid growing up in the '60s, your bicycle was like your right arm—you wouldn't know what to do without it. No matter how old or new, whether it was a hand-me-down, repainted and loved again, or a brand-new birthday bike, we all loved to push those pedals and ride, ride, ride! One autumn afternoon, my dad took an old deck of cards from the game closet, grabbed Mom's clothespin bag, and called the three of us kids to the sidewalk in front of our house. Working on each of our bicycles, he attached the playing cards to the spokes with the clothespins, and then told us to hop on our bikes and ride like the wind. The clatter that came from our bikes was magnificent! The faster we rode, the louder the noise, and we all swore our bikes sounded just like motorcycles.

As I was making this quilt, it reminded me of those cards on the spokes, and I couldn't help but smile at the memories. I hope making this quilt will make you smile as well.

3. Repeat to make 2 strip sets each in the following combinations: cream/blue, cream/green, yellow/pink, yellow/blue, peach/green, and peach/eggplant. Open and starch each strip set as described in "Starch for Success" on page 11.

Make 4.

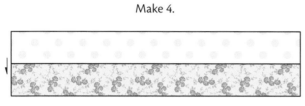

Make 2.

Make 2.

Make 2.

Make 2.

Make 2.

Make 2.

Cutting and Organizing the Triangles

1. Referring to "Cutting Triangles" on page 11, cut six 90° double-strip triangles from each strip set. Cut each triangle in half to make two smaller, mirror-image triangles as instructed in "Sub-Cutting Triangles" on page 13.

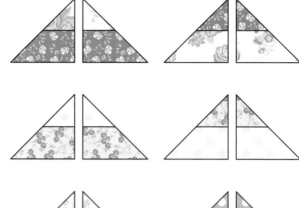
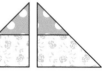
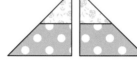
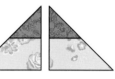
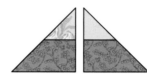
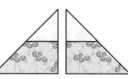
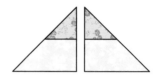
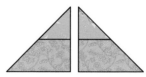

2. Separate the triangles into 28 sets of:
   - 12 cream tip/pink strip pointing left
   - 12 cream tip/pink strip pointing right
   - 12 pink tip/cream strip pointing left
   - 12 pink tip/cream strip pointing right
   - 6 cream tip/blue strip pointing left
   - 6 cream tip/blue strip pointing right
   - 6 blue tip/cream strip pointing left
   - 6 blue tip/cream strip pointing right
   - 6 cream tip/green strip pointing left
   - 6 cream tip/green strip pointing right
   - 6 green tip/cream strip pointing left
   - 6 green tip/cream strip pointing right
   - 6 yellow tip/pink strip pointing left
   - 6 yellow tip/pink strip pointing right
   - 6 pink tip/yellow strip pointing left
   - 6 pink tip/yellow strip pointing right
   - 6 yellow tip/blue strip pointing left
   - 6 yellow tip/blue strip pointing right
   - 6 blue tip/yellow strip pointing left
   - 6 blue tip/yellow strip pointing right
   - 6 peach tip/green strip pointing left
   - 6 peach tip/green strip pointing right
   - 6 green tip/peach tip pointing left
   - 6 green tip/peach tip pointing right
   - 6 peach tip/eggplant strip pointing left
   - 6 peach tip/eggplant strip pointing right
   - 6 eggplant tip/peach strip pointing left
   - 6 eggplant tip/peach strip pointing right

Constructing the Blocks

Refer to the illustrations at right and arrange the triangles on a design wall or other flat surface to ensure correct placement prior to sewing.

1. With right sides together, sew a cream tip/pink strip pointing left triangle to a cream tip/blue strip pointing left triangle. Repeat to make a second triangle unit. Sew these two units together to make a block. Repeat to make a total of 3 blocks. Starch each block to preserve the bias edges of the triangles.

Make 3.

2. Repeat with two cream tip/pink strip pointing right triangles and two cream tip/blue strip pointing right triangles to make a block. Make a total of 3 blocks.

Make 3.

3. Repeat to make 3 of each block shown below, for a total of 48 blocks.

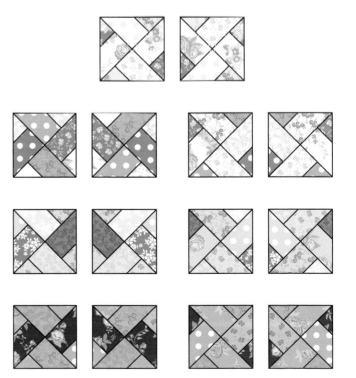

Assembling the Quilt Top

1. Using a design wall or other flat surface, arrange the completed blocks as shown.
2. Sew the blocks in each row together; press the seam allowances in opposite directions from row to row. Sew the rows together; press the seam allowances in one direction. To stabilize the bias edges of the quilt top, stitch around the perimeter ⅛" from the raw edges.

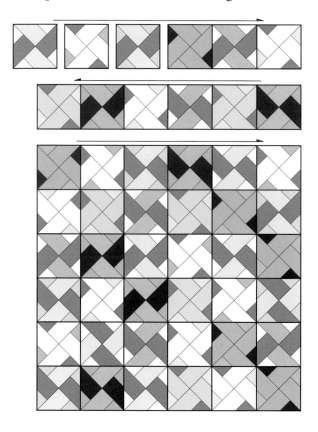

Adding the Borders

1. Referring to "Adding Borders" on page 14, join two inner-border strips to make one long strip. Repeat to make another pieced strip. Sew the pieced inner-border strips to the right and left edges of the quilt top; press. Sew the single border strips to the top and bottom edges; press.
2. Join two outer-border strips to make one long strip. Repeat to make a total of four pieced strips. Add the outer-border strips to the quilt top.

Finishing

1. Referring to "Completing the Quilt" on page 14, layer the quilt top with batting and backing. Quilt as desired.
2. Follow the instructions on page 15 to bind the quilt using the 2½"-wide strips.

Box Hockey

Designed by Kathy Brown; pieced by the Southern Ladies Quilting Society; quilted by Carol Hilton

Finished Quilt: 59" x 70" ★ Finished Block: 5½" x 5½"

Materials

Yardage is based on 42"-wide fabric.

2 fat quarters of assorted purple prints for blocks
2 fat quarters of assorted gold prints for blocks
2 fat quarters of assorted black prints for blocks
3 fat quarters of assorted navy prints for blocks
3 fat quarters of assorted green prints for blocks
4 fat quarters of assorted red prints for blocks
2½ yards of natural muslin for blocks
¾ yard of gold print for inner border
2⅛ yards of navy print for outer border
   and binding
4¼ yards of fabric for backing
67" x 78" piece of batting

Cutting

From the fat quarters of assorted purple prints, cut a total of:
8 strips, 2½" x 21"

From the fat quarters of assorted gold prints, cut a total of:
8 strips, 2½" x 21"

From the fat quarters of assorted black prints, cut a total of:
8 strips, 2½" x 21"

From the fat quarters of assorted navy prints, cut a total of:
12 strips, 2½" x 21"

From the fat quarters of assorted green prints, cut a total of:
12 strips, 2½" x 21"

From the fat quarters of assorted red prints, cut a total of:
14 strips, 2½" x 21"

From the muslin, cut:
31 strips, 2½" x 42"; cut each strip in half to yield
   62 strips, each 21" long

As kids, every summer we would sign up for the box-hockey tournaments at our neighborhood park. Box hockey was my favorite of all the park activities and quite a challenging sport. A large rectangular wooden box, two "hockey" sticks (wheelbarrow handles made of wood), a croquet ball, and two willing participants were all we needed for a frenzied game to begin. Many a bruised shin or forearm was acquired in the process and worn with pride over a battle well fought. More lasting than the bruises, however, were the recollections of summer days, friendships forged in battle, and a lifetime of memories to be relived. This quilt brings back those box-hockey tournaments, when our sticks were crossed in unison at the start of each game.

From the gold print, cut:
8 inner-border strips, 2½" x 42"

From the navy print, cut:
8 outer-border strips, 6" x 42"
8 binding strips, 2½" x 42"

Constructing the Blocks

1. With right sides together, sew a colored strip to a muslin strip. Repeat to make a total of 62 colored print/muslin strip sets. Open and starch each strip set as described in "Starch for Success" on page 11.

Make 8.

Make 8.

Make 8.

Make 8.

Make 8.

Make 8.

2. Referring to "Cutting Triangles" on page 11, cut three 90° double-strip triangles from each strip set.

3. Separate the triangles into 12 sets of:
   - 12 purple print tip/muslin strip
   - 12 muslin tip/purple print strip
   - 12 gold print tip/muslin strip*
   - 12 muslin tip/gold print strip
   - 12 black print tip/muslin strip
   - 12 muslin tip/black print strip
   - 18 navy print tip/muslin strip*
   - 18 muslin tip/navy print strip*
   - 18 green print tip/muslin strip*
   - 18 muslin tip/green print strip*
   - 21 red print tip/muslin strip*
   - 21 muslin tip/red print strip*

All other triangles are extra and can be used for another project.

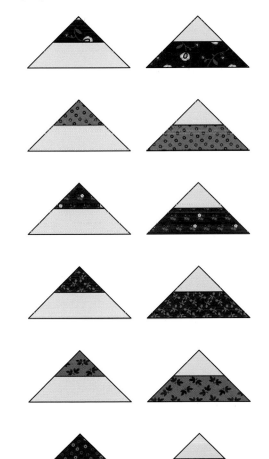

4. With right sides together, sew a purple print–tip triangle to a muslin tip/green print strip triangle. Repeat to make a total of 12 blocks.

Make 12.

5. Using the triangle combinations shown in the illustrations below, repeat to make the number of blocks specified for each combination, for a total of 80 blocks. Starch each block to preserve the bias edges of the triangles.

Make 16.

Make 16.

Make 12.

Make 12.

Make 8.

Make 4.

Assembling the Quilt Top

1. Using a design wall or other flat surface, arrange the completed blocks as shown.
2. Sew the blocks in each row together; press the seam allowances in opposite directions from row to row. Sew the rows together; press the seam allowances in one direction. To stabilize the bias edges of the quilt top, stitch around the perimeter ⅛" from the raw edges.

Adding the Borders

1. Referring to "Adding Borders" on page 14, join two inner-border strips to make one long strip. Repeat to make a total of four pieced strips. Sew the inner-border strips to the quilt top; press.
2. Repeat to add the outer-border strips to the quilt top.

Finishing

1. Referring to "Completing the Quilt" on page 14, layer the quilt top with batting and backing. Quilt as desired.
2. Follow the instructions on page 15 to bind the quilt using the 2½"-wide strips.

Romeo and Juliet

Designed by Kathy Brown; pieced by Linda Reed; quilted by Carol Hilton

Finished Quilt: 54" x 70" ★ Finished Block: 8" x 8"

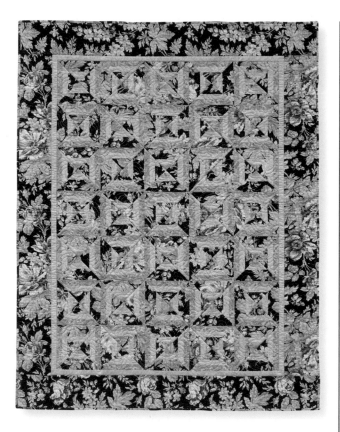

Materials

Yardage is based on 42"-wide fabric.

1½ yards of blue tone-on-tone fabric for blocks and inner border

1¼ yards of pink paisley fabric for blocks

3½ yards of large-scale black floral for blocks, outer border, and binding

4 yards of fabric for backing

62" x 78" piece of batting

Cutting

From the pink paisley fabric, cut:
24 strips, 1½" x 42"

From the blue tone-on-tone fabric, cut:
24 strips, 1½" x 42"
8 inner-border strips, 1½" x 42"

From the large-scale black floral, cut:
24 strips, 2½" x 42"
8 outer-border strips, 6½" x 42"
8 binding strips, 2½" x 42"

Constructing the Blocks

1. With right sides together, sew a pink paisley strip, a blue tone-on-tone strip, and a large-scale black floral strip into a strip set as shown. Repeat to make a total of 24 pink/blue/black strip sets. Open and starch each strip set as described in "Starch for Success" on page 11.

Make 24.

I was 13 when Romeo and Juliet *took to the big screen, with Olivia Hussey and Leonard Whiting as the star-crossed lovers. My girlfriends and I wanted to see the tragic tale, and for the first time in our young-adult lives our mothers allowed us to go downtown to the big theater, be dropped off by ourselves, and be totally captivated for two glorious hours. For impressionable young girls, this was the epitome of true love and a Saturday afternoon that would live in our hearts forever.*

When I came upon this beautiful floral fabric, I was instantly reminded of that Saturday afternoon years ago. The blocks as they are pieced, same yet different, strike a chord with me and bring to mind the fated couple, united forever in love. It's the perfect lap quilt to snuggle under with a good book or a romantic movie!

2. Referring to "Cutting Triangles" on page 11, cut six 90° triple-strip triangles from each strip set.

3. Separate the triangles into two sets of 72 triangles each:
   - pink tip/blue strip/black strip
   - black tip/blue strip/pink strip

4. With right sides together, sew a pink-tip triangle to a black-tip triangle. Repeat to make a second unit.

5. With right sides together, sew the two units together. Repeat to make a total of 35 blocks. (Note: You'll have four triangles left over.) Starch each block to preserve the bias edges of the triangles.

Make 24.

Assembling the Quilt Top

1. Using a design wall or other flat surface, arrange the completed blocks as shown. *Author's note:* The quilt assembly diagram shows the placement of the blocks as they're intended to be. However, I just had to break the rules and piece this quilt a little differently. Can you spot the difference in the photo?

2. Sew the blocks in each row together; press the seam allowances in opposite directions from row to row. Sew the rows together; press the seam allowances in one direction. To stabilize the bias edges of the quilt top, stitch around the perimeter ⅛" from the raw edges.

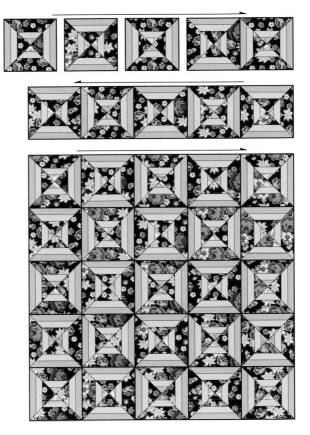

Adding the Borders

1. Referring to "Adding Borders" on page 14, join two inner-border strips to make one long strip. Repeat to make a total of four pieced strips. Sew the inner-border strips to the quilt top; press.

2. Repeat to add the outer-border strips to the quilt top.

Finishing

1. Referring to "Completing the Quilt" on page 14, layer the quilt top with batting and backing. Quilt as desired.

2. Follow the instructions on page 15 to bind the quilt using the 2½"-wide strips.

Penny Candy

Designed by Kathy Brown; pieced by Linda Reed and Janell Crosslin; quilted by Carol Hilton

Finished Quilt: 72" x 80" ★ Finished Block: 8" x 8"

Every summer, Mom would pick a day and announce that we were "going downtown!" Downtown Baton Rouge was a magical place for kids, a concrete jungle of tall buildings, outdoor sculptures, museums, theaters, multilevel department stores (which meant we got to ride escalators!), and drugstore soda fountains. On this day, my dad would line us up in the den before he left for work and give us his speech about minding our manners. He would then reach deep into his pocket and pull out a dollar bill for each one of us. In those days, a dollar could stretch pretty darn far in a five-and-dime store, and invariably the three of us would save our dollars for lots of penny candy!

When searching for fabric for this quilt, I came across these luscious colors that reminded me of special summer days filled with the wonders of downtown and penny candy. I hope this quilt will remind you of carefree summer days too.

Materials

Yardage is based on 42"-wide fabric.

4 fat quarters of assorted butter yellow prints for blocks

4 fat quarters of assorted mint green prints for blocks

4 fat quarters of assorted cotton-candy pink prints for blocks

4 fat quarters of assorted sky blue prints for blocks

4 fat quarters of assorted cherry red prints for blocks

3¾ yards of white-tone-on tone fabric for blocks and binding

¾ yard of cherry red print for inner border

1¾ yards of sky blue print for outer border

4⅞ yards of fabric for backing

80" x 88" piece of batting

Cutting

From *each* of the 20 fat quarters, cut:
4 strips, 2½" x 21"

From the white tone-on-tone fabric, cut:
40 strips, 2½" x 42"; cut each strip in half to yield 80 strips, each 21" long
8 binding strips, 2½" x 42"

From the cherry red print, cut:
8 inner-border strips, 2½" x 42"

From the sky blue print, cut:
8 outer-border strips, 6½" x 42"

Constructing the Blocks

1. With right sides together, sew a colored strip to a white tone-on-tone strip. Repeat to make a total of 16 strip sets from each color grouping of fat-quarter strips. Open and starch each strip set as described in "Starch for Success" on page 11.

Make 16.

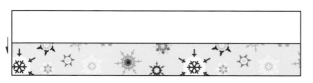

Make 16.

Make 16.

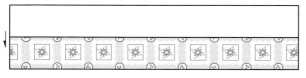

Make16.

Make 16.

2. Referring to "Cutting Triangles" on page 11, cut three 90° double-strip triangles from each strip set.

3. Separate the triangles into 10 sets of 24 triangles each:
   - butter yellow tip/white strip
   - white tip/butter yellow strip
   - mint green tip/white strip
   - white tip/mint green strip
   - cotton-candy pink tip/white strip
   - white tip/cotton-candy pink strip
   - sky blue tip/white strip
   - white tip/sky blue strip
   - cherry red tip/white strip
   - white tip/cherry red strip

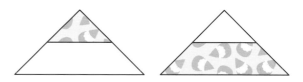

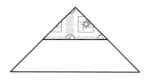
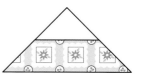
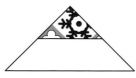

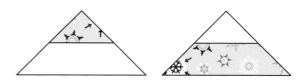

4. With right sides together, sew a butter yellow–tip triangle to a white tip/butter yellow–strip triangle. Repeat to make a second unit. With right sides together, join the units. Repeat to make a total of 12 butter yellow/white blocks.

Make 12.

5. Repeat to make a total of 11 mint green/white blocks, 11 cotton-candy pink/white blocks, 11 sky blue/white blocks, and 11 cherry red/white blocks. You'll have 16 triangles left over. Starch each block to preserve the bias edges of the triangles.

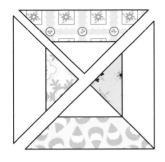

Make 11.

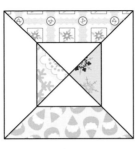

Make 11.

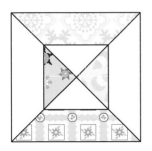

Make 11.

Make 11.

Assembling the Quilt Top

1. Using a design wall or other flat surface, arrange the completed blocks as shown.

2. Sew the blocks in each row together; press the seam allowances in opposite directions from row to row. Sew the rows together; press the seam allowances in one direction. To stabilize the bias edges of the quilt top, stitch around the perimeter ⅛" from the raw edges.

Adding the Borders

1. Referring to "Adding Borders" on page 14, join two inner-border strips to make one long strip. Repeat to make a total of four pieced strips. Sew the inner-border strips to the quilt top; press.

2. Repeat to add the outer-border strips to the quilt top.

Finishing

1. Referring to "Completing the Quilt" on page 14, layer the quilt top with batting and backing. Quilt as desired.

2. Follow the instructions on page 15 to bind the quilt using the 2½"-wide strips.

Family Vacation

Designed by Kathy Brown; pieced by Linda Reed; quilted by Carol Hilton

Finished Quilt: 52" x 62½" ★ Finished Block: 10½" x 10½"

One of my favorite comedies is Family Vacation, where Clark Griswold takes the kids and mom on a summer vacation in the trusty family station wagon. It reminds me of the hours spent in the back of our Rambler, heading to destinations like Florida, where we played for hours in the crystal-clear waters of the Gulf of Mexico and collected seashells along the sugar-white sandy beaches. On one of those trips, when I was nine, my dad held my hand as we waded out until the water was waist deep on me. It wasn't long before a school of dolphins passed by, and we were able to reach out and touch several as they brushed past our legs. The experience was a thrill and is most likely the reason I love the gulf coast so much. As I pulled together the fabrics for this quilt, they reminded me of that special dolphin encounter, and the wonderful memories of family vacations gone by.

Materials

Yardage is based on 42"-wide fabric.

¾ yard *each* of 4 blue batiks
¾ yard *each* of 4 purple batiks
2 yards of multicolored floral batik for border and binding
3⅓ yards of fabric for backing (pieced with a horizontal backing)
60" x 71" piece of batting

Cutting

From *each* of the 4 blue batiks, cut:
14 strips, 1½" x 42" (56 total)

From *each* of the 4 purple batiks, cut:
14 strips, 1½" x 42" (56 total)

From the multicolored floral batik, cut:
8 outer-border strips, 5½" x 42"
8 binding strips, 2½" x 42"

Assembling the Strip Sets

With right sides together, make a strip set alternating two different blue and two different purple strips. Make 28 strip sets. Open and starch each strip set as described in "Starch for Success" on page 11.

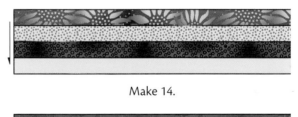

Make 14.

Make 14.

Cutting and Organizing the Triangles

1. Referring to "Cutting Triangles" on page 11, cut six 90° multi-strip triangles from each strip set. Cut each triangle in half to make two smaller, mirror-image triangles as instructed in "Sub-Cutting Triangles" on page 13.

2. Separate the triangles into 4 sets and label them A, B, C, and D.

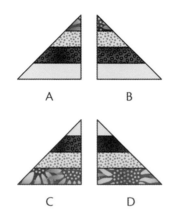

Constructing the Blocks

Refer to the illustrations below and at right and place the triangles on a design wall or other flat surface to ensure correct placement prior to sewing.

1. With right sides together, sew an A triangle to a D triangle, orienting the triangles as shown. Follow with a D triangle to an A triangle. Sew the AD unit to the DA unit to make a square. Repeat to make a total of 40 AD squares.

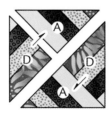 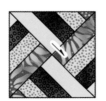

Make 40.

2. With right sides together, sew a B triangle to a C triangle. Follow with a C triangle to a B triangle. Sew the BC unit to the CB unit to make a square. Repeat to make a total of 40 BC squares. Starch each square to preserve the bias edges of the triangles. Note: You'll have a total of 16 triangles left over.

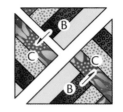 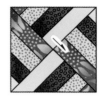

Make 40.

3. With right sides together, sew a BC square to an AD square. Sew an AD square to a BC square. Sew the two units together to make a Four Patch block. Repeat to make a total of 20 blocks.

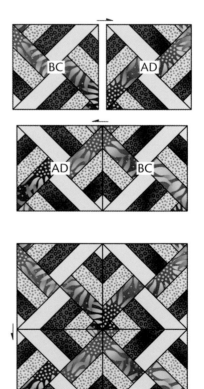

Make 20.

Assembling the Quilt Top

1. Using a design wall or other flat surface, arrange the completed blocks as shown.
2. Sew the blocks in each row together; press the seam allowances in opposite directions from row to row. Sew the rows together; press the seam allowances in one direction. To stabilize the bias edges of the quilt top, stitch around the perimeter ⅛" from the raw edges.

Adding the Borders

Referring to "Adding Borders" on page 14, join two border strips to make one long strip. Repeat to make a total of four pieced strips. Sew the border strips to the quilt top; press.

Finishing

1. Referring to "Completing the Quilt" on page 14, layer the quilt top with batting and backing. Quilt as desired.
2. Follow the instructions on page 15 to bind the quilt using the 2½"-wide strips.

Cupsicles

Designed by Kathy Brown; pieced by the Southern Ladies Quilting Society; quilted by Carol Hilton

Finished Quilt: 55" x 77" ★ Finished Block: 11" x 11"

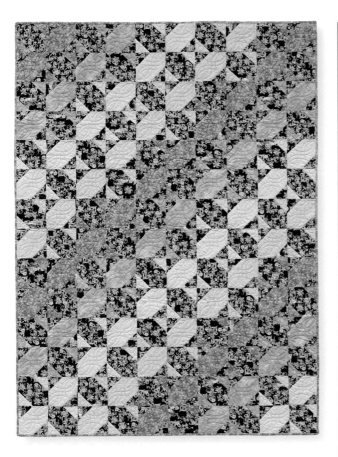

Materials

Yardage is based on 42"-wide fabric.

1⅔ yards of orange crush fabric for blocks
    and binding
1 yard *each* of blue raspberry, pineapple yellow,
    and lemon-lime green fabrics for blocks
3¾ yards of black floral for blocks
4¾ yards of fabric for backing
63" x 85" piece of batting

Cutting

From the orange crush fabric, cut:
12 strips, 2½" x 42"
8 binding strips, 2½" x 42"

From the blue raspberry fabric, cut:
12 strips, 2½" x 42"

From the pineapple yellow fabric, cut:
12 strips, 2½" x 42"

From the lemon-lime green fabric, cut:
12 strips, 2½" x 42"

From the black floral, cut:
48 strips, 2½" x 42"

"We're going on vacation!" *My brothers and I loved family vacations, but the allowances we earned for household chores were never enough to fund our vacation spending. It was up to us to devise a get-rich-quick plan! Living across the street from the local ballpark provided the perfect opportunity. From late afternoon until way after dark every summer night, the local youth softball and baseball leagues played in the oppressive heat and humidity, and while they played, the fans sat in the stands and sweltered. With help from Mom, we made gallons of sweet, fruity Kool-Aid, filled Dixie cups, and froze the icy treats. A large ice chest loaded into our red wagon and a homemade poster announcing "Cupsicles – 5 cents" were all we needed to stuff our piggy banks!*

The colors in this quilt remind me of those hot summer nights and icy Kool-Aid treats. I hope you'll enjoy making this quilty cupsicle.

Constructing the Blocks

1. With right sides together, sew a colored strip to a black floral strip. Repeat to make 12 strips sets in each combination. Open and starch each strip set as described in "Starch for Success" on page 11.

Make 12.

Make 12.

Make 12.

Make 12.

2. Referring to "Cutting Triangles" on page 11, cut six 90° double-strip triangles from each strip set.

3. Separate the triangles into 8 sets of 36 triangles each:
   - orange tip/black floral strip
   - black floral tip/orange strip
   - blue tip/black floral strip
   - black floral tip/blue strip
   - yellow tip/black floral strip
   - black floral tip/yellow strip
   - green tip/black floral strip
   - black floral tip/green strip

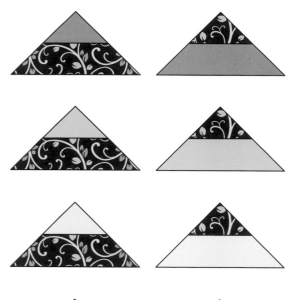

4. With right sides together, sew a black floral tip/orange strip triangle to another black floral tip/orange strip triangle. Repeat to make a total of 18 squares.

Make 18.

5. With right sides together, sew an orange-tip triangle to another orange-tip triangle. Repeat to make a total of 18 squares.

Make 18.

6. From the remaining sets of triangles, make the number of squares indicated below. (Note: You'll have 8 triangles left over.) Starch each square to preserve the bias edges of the triangles.

Make 18.   Make 18.

Make 18.   Make 18.

Make 16.   Make 16.

7. With right sides together, join two orange/black squares as shown. Repeat to make a second unit. Join the units to make a block. Repeat to make 9 blocks.

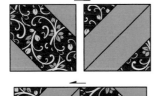 

Make 9.

8. Repeat to make 9 blue/black blocks, 9 yellow/black blocks, and 8 green/black blocks.

Assembling the Quilt Top

1. Using a design wall or other flat surface, arrange the completed blocks as shown below, making sure that each block is oriented with the black floral strips flowing from the upper-left corner to the lower-right corner of the quilt top, and the colored strips flowing from the lower-left corner to the upper-right corner.

2. Sew the blocks in each row together; press the seam allowances in opposite directions from row to row. Sew the rows together; press the seam allowances in one direction. To stabilize the bias edges of the quilt top, stitch around the perimeter ⅛" from the raw edges.

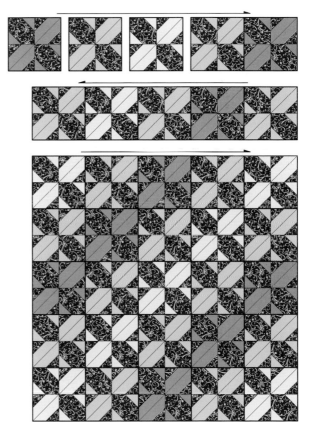

Finishing

1. Referring to "Completing the Quilt" on page 14, layer the quilt top with batting and backing. Quilt as desired.

2. Follow the instructions on page 15 to bind the quilt using the 2½"-wide strips.

Pick Up Sticks

Designed by Kathy Brown; pieced by Linda Reed; quilted by Carol Hilton

Finished Quilt: 49" x 60" ★ Finished Block: 5½" x 5½"

Pick Up Sticks was one of my all-time favorite games to play. I loved the way the thin sticks would fall into a colorful heap, and the skill required to remove one without the others shifting. This quilt brings back all of the fun of Pick Up Sticks, without the tension and stress that went along with carefully trying not to move another stick! Part of the fun is in choosing your fat quarters for the quilt—and challenging yourself to make them as scrappy as can be.

Materials

Yardage is based on 42"-wide fabric.

3 fat quarters of assorted gold prints for blocks and outer border*

3 fat quarters of assorted orange prints for blocks and outer border

3 fat quarters of assorted navy prints for blocks and outer border

3 fat quarters of assorted green prints for blocks and outer border

3 fat quarters of assorted red prints for blocks and outer border

3⅓ yards of natural muslin for blocks, inner border, and binding

3¼ yards of fabric for backing (pieced with a horizontal seam)

57" x 78" piece of batting

The fat quarters in each group can be the same color, but the quilt will be scrappier if you choose different prints.

Cutting

From the gold fat quarters, cut a *total* of:
12 strips, 2½" x 21"

From the orange fat quarters, cut a *total* of:
12 strips, 2½" x 21"

From the navy fat quarters, cut a *total* of:
12 strips, 2½" x 21"

From the green fat quarters, cut a *total* of:
12 strips, 2½" x 21"

From the red fat quarters, cut a *total* of:
12 strips, 2½" x 21"

From the muslin, cut:
30 strips, 2½" x 42"; cut *each* strip in half to yield 60 strips, 2½" x 21"
8 binding strips, 2½" x 42"
8 inner-border strips, 1½" x 42"

From the remaining gold, orange, navy, green, and red fat quarters (your choice), cut a *total* of:
12 outer-border strips, 3" x 21"

Constructing the Blocks

1. With right sides together, sew a colored strip to a muslin strip. Repeat to make a total of 60 colored/muslin strip sets. Open and starch each strip set as described in "Starch for Success" on page 11.

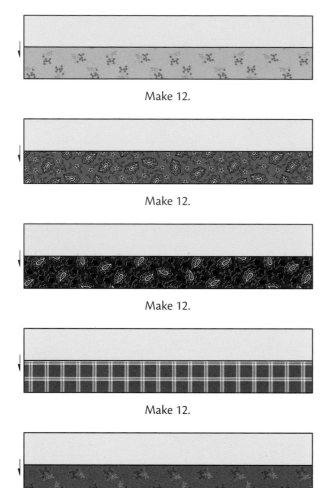

Make 12.

Make 12.

Make 12.

Make 12.

Make 12.

2. Referring to "Cutting Triangles" on page 11, cut three 90° double-strip triangles from each strip set.

3. Separate the triangles into two sets of 90 triangles each:
   - muslin tip/colored strip
   - colored tip/muslin strip

4. With right sides together, sew a muslin-tip triangle to a colored-tip triangle to make a block. The colored strip and tip in the two triangles can be the same print, but should be a different color. Repeat to make a total of 80 assorted blocks. (Note: You'll have 20 triangles left over.) Starch each block to preserve the bias edges of the triangles.

Make 80
assorted blocks.

Assembling the Quilt Top

1. Using a design wall or other flat surface, arrange the completed blocks as shown. This quilt is meant to be scrappy, so distribute the colors randomly across the surface and avoid having the same colors touch.
2. Sew the blocks in each row together; press the seam allowances in opposite directions from row to row. Sew the rows together; press the seam allowances in one direction. To stabilize the bias edges of the quilt top, stitch around the perimeter ⅛" from the raw edges.

Adding the Borders

1. Referring to "Adding Borders" on page 14, join two inner-border strips to make one long strip. Repeat to make a total of four pieced strips. Sew the inner-border strips to the quilt top; press.
2. Join three colored outer-border strips to make one long strip, sewing the ends straight together rather than on the diagonal as you did with the inner borders. Repeat to make a total of four pieced strips. Sew the outer-border strips to the quilt top.

Finishing

1. Referring to "Completing the Quilt" on page 14, layer the quilt top with batting and backing. Quilt as desired.
2. Follow the instructions on page 15 to bind the quilt using the 2½"-wide strips.

Acknowledgments

With a grateful heart, I give warm thanks to:
The quilters who helped pull these fabrics
together and make beautiful quilts:

The Southern Ladies Quilting Society: Cheryl
Wilks, Ann Reily, Janell Crosslin, Denise Bayer,
Andrea Keith, Yvonne Smode, Wanda Hoffman,
Mynan Guidry, and especially Linda Reed for
pulling together in troubled times and getting
these quilts made *tout de suite*! I'm so grateful for
your generosity and your friendship. Thank you
just doesn't seem adequate.

Pam Vieira-McGinnis for taking on the challenge of a new ruler with a new technique and
coming through like a champ! You're the best!

Carol Hilton for waving her magic wand and
getting these quilts quilted in record time! I'm
honored to be one of your clients.

The wonderful, generous folks at Andover,
Hoffman Fabrics, Lecien Fabrics, Moda, and
Studio e Fabrics for supplying the fabrics used in
these quilts.

Moda Lissa for jumping through hoops for
me each and every time I bugged the heck out of
her for "just a little more fabric"!

Rob Kreiger of Checker Distributors for his
generous and unwavering support as I dove into
the world of Creative Grid Rulers, and Nancy
Weber for her leadership and guidance in the last
15 years. I have been blessed with the gift of her
friendship.

And last but not least, Karen, Cathy, Mary,
Christine, and the rest of the fabulous staff at
Martingale & Company for their help in pulling
this book together. I feel so privileged to have the
opportunity to work with you!

About the Author

As I sit here writing this, it's 101° outside on a sweltering August afternoon, and I just have to laugh. What's a southern Louisiana girl like me doing in a place like this? Quilting? In this heat? Quilting and the heat and humidity of Louisiana seem to go together like oil and water. But here I sit, loving each and every minute of it as I have for the past 16 years. And if the creeks don't rise and the rains don't fall, I'll be at it for a very long time to come!

In addition to sitting at the sewing machine, I'm privileged to design fabric for Red Rooster Fabrics. Imagine that—getting an idea for fabrics that I'd like to quilt with, taking those images out of my head, putting them down on paper, painting them, shipping them off, and months later, turning those images into beautiful quilts when the fabric arrives. Fortunate indeed!

Beyond the quilting and the painting, I'm a mom to the best daughter anyone could ever hope for, wife of 34 years to my wonderful best friend Michael, and doggie/kitty mom to six loving cats, two fantastic German Shepherds, a spunky Welsh Corgi, and an incredible Catahoula. This is the life!

THERE'S MORE ONLINE!

See an array of Kathy's patterns, read her blog, and learn about her workshops and lectures at www.the-teachers-pet.com.

You might also enjoy these other fine titles from
Martingale & Company

Our books are available at bookstores and your favorite craft, fabric, and yarn retailers.
Visit us at www.martingale-pub.com or contact us at:

1-800-426-3126
International: 1-425-483-3313
Fax: 1-425-486-7596
Email: info@martingale-pub.com

Martingale®
& COMPANY

America's Best-Loved Craft & Hobby Books®
America's Best-Loved Knitting Books®

That Patchwork Place®

America's Best-Loved Quilt Books®